Inside the Dark

Holden Reyes

Inside the Dark

Olympia Publishers
London

www.olympiapublishers.com
OLYMPIA PAPERBACK EDITION

Copyright © Holden Reyes 2023

The right of Holden Reyes to be identified as author of
this work has been asserted in accordance with sections 77 and 78 of
the Copyright, Designs and Patents Act 1988.

All Rights Reserved

No reproduction, copy or transmission of this publication
may be made without written permission.
No paragraph of this publication may be reproduced,
copied or transmitted save with the written permission of the publisher,
or in accordance with the provisions
of the Copyright Act 1956 (as amended).

Any person who commits any unauthorised act in relation to
this publication may be liable to criminal
prosecution and civil claims for damage.

A CIP catalogue record for this title is
available from the British Library.

ISBN: 978-1-80439-408-3

This is a work of fiction.
Names, characters, places and incidents originate from the writer's
imagination. Any resemblance to actual persons, living or dead, is
purely coincidental.

First Published in 2023

**Olympia Publishers
Tallis House
2 Tallis Street
London
EC4Y 0AB**

Printed in Great Britain

Acknowledgements

Thank you for taking the time to read "Inside the Dark". For the last twenty years on my life, I have had to hide my true self. I have had to hide myself under perfectionism. Because if you look perfect, do perfect, and accomplish perfect, you would minimize the shame, judgement, and regret you put upon yourself. This book is only the beginning for me and that's scary. I am not sure where I will be or what I will become after this but I am grateful. Grateful for being able to share this part of me with you. Grateful for being able to change my life one step at a time. And grateful for the opportunity to have what I want in this life. This shows the results of the many years hiding in the shadows without knowing who I was. Thank you for allowing me to share this part of me with you.

Have you ever wondered what kind of life you would have if you didn't give in to the "norms" of society? Well, this book represents that idea but focuses on the darkness that comes from dealing with the norms of society, and the need of wanting to be true to who you are as an individual. This is a coming-of-age book. This book is about the last twenty years of my life and how I have been hiding my true self. It explores the back-and-forth emotions and experiences of love, heartbreak, and healing.

Inside of the dark, there is nothing. It's simply empty. I have hidden inside not knowing who I was, who I wanted to become, or how to be my true self. This book will consist of thoughts, quotes, and poetry highlighting some hardships of living with depression, anxiety, and the effects it has on relationships with yourself and loved ones. This book is for those who are lost inside the dark wanting to escape the idea of norms in society and wanting to live a life without regret but feeling as if they will not succeed. For years, I have hidden inside the dark not knowing who I was and this represents the effects of that.

You're not alone.

I have tried so hard
To be the person I want to be.

But being different,

I feel as if
I will never be
Who they want me to be,
Regardless of who I am inside.

At times,

I hold my breath.
I hold my breath when I can't be who I am.

I am dead inside,
Smiling from the outside
Wondering if anyone
Will ever notice.

It's been decades.

Decades of:
Lying,
Sadness,
Trauma,
And misery.

It's been decades and I still can't be me.

Every day I hide.

I hide my
True emotions

And

Still wonder why
I can't be free
From my inner thoughts.

If my inner thoughts could speak,
They would tell me to run.

To run as fast as I can and never look back.
I would be free to be who I am
And who I am meant to be.

I'm scared.
Scared to let you inside.
To show you what I have been hiding all of these years.
But if I did let you in,
I would be free from my thoughts.

I push away those
Who have my best interests at heart.
Why?
Because I am not the person, they think I am.
I am living in a world where I am stuck
Inside hiding from myself.

My dreams cause me harm.
Not because they are filled with death, pain, or hardship.
But because they are filled with ambition and happiness.
I am happier in my dreams than in reality.

I wake up
And realize
Who I want to become.

But the darkness has taken over my life.
It has taken my passion and my future.
I do not think I can find the light
In my life.

It may just be too late.

I dream
Of light
Shining in my face.

I dream of a life
That takes the darkness,
And
Turns it into light.

Most nights I don't sleep.

I think of you
And how I may never have you.

I stand in my room,
In the dark,
And realize I may not be enough.

I have let myself down.
I feel I cannot escape this darkness in my life.
I am sitting here,
Realizing, I have nothing.

No person.
No one to be there when I need them.
All I have is an empty suitcase,
Waiting to be filled.

Their mistake was falling for me.

Falling for a guy,
Who is enclosed in darkness
Waiting to find himself.

Waiting to realize
That his room
Cannot always be there
For him to hide in.

The death of me
Is the silent killer,
Known as memories.

Creeping up unannounced
Disguising themselves as innocent

Knowing they intend to do harm.

I'm empty inside.
I'm not happy.

I have hidden for so long.
I feel as if I can't ever be the real me.

I have hidden myself from every living thing
That I have learned to smile through the pain.

To hide every day
Is another knife in my heart.

Not knowing what to do,
Is the worst sadness I have ever experienced.

There's an empty parking lot
Where I go
To look up at the moon,
To ask myself
Where I went wrong.

I am tying my best to be okay
But every day is a constant battle with my emotions.
Fighting a war that I will inevitably lose.
So, I hold my breath
Till I can let go
And say those three words
I have been dying to say my whole life.

"I Love Myself"

I look at the ocean with jealousy
Because of how free it seems to be.
It's boundless.
And for how it didn't change,
Whether you love it or hate it.

I find myself jealous.
Jealous of the lives I see that are happy
And loving the world we are in.

Jealous of the thought's ones can express out loud
Versus
Mine, where I hide deep in my soul.

Simply jealous that I can't have what they have.
Jealous of their existence.

Sometimes it's hard.

Hard to know
What you really want
And what you need.

The difference?

I'm not even sure,
But I'll let you know when I find it.

All I want is to
To find a star in a galaxy
That is filled with billions of stars.
But just like other stars, I have collapsed.
Now I'm in a galaxy by myself,
Surrounded and trapped
 By darkness.

There is a difference between being happy
Then being distracted from sadness.
And after hearing that,
It really does make you rethink
Some of the things that
Make you happy. I lie awake at night.

Thinking of where I could have been.

Where I could be
If I didn't give in to society.

I could have been happy.

I have been struggling for a while now.

Struggling with the thoughts, emotions, and ideas,
That I have buried inside my mind.

Struggling,
Trying to overcome these feelings
But feel as if I never will.

I'm Lost.

Lost in a world, full or regret.

I have gotten through the years by
Smiling on the outside, and
Dying on the inside.

Now I'm stuck in the in-between.

Emptiness is all I feel.

I wish I could rewind my life and start over.

If I could, I still don't think I would be myself.

I'm too good at hiding my true self.

Standing on a bridge
In the dark.

Waiting for the darkness to shine.

But,

There is never any light on this bridge.

I stand here,
In the dark.
With my thoughts filled full of fear and resentment.

Fear of myself wanting to be happy,
And resentment upon the idea of wanting to be happy.

Everyone always asks,
"What's wrong?"

If I told them,
I don't think they would even stick around.

Maybe I live in fear.

Not because people might not love me for me.

But because of what they would say about me.

I have spent years hiding.

Hiding from my thoughts,
Perceived by what I really want.

Hiding, because it's what I am best at.

Nobody is worth
Letting go of what you need to be happy.

I am the
Only person
Who can open that door.

Nothing is more dangerous,
Than smiling through all the pain and self-doubt.

Hurting someone's feelings
Is like throwing a rock
Into the ocean,

But you will never know how deep that rock goes.

My emotions are buried
Inside my soul.

So far deep,
They will never find
Their true potential.

When we struggle, we struggle for a while.

Struggle with the thoughts, emotions, and ideas that we have buried inside our minds.

We struggle and try to overcome these feelings but feel as if we never will.

I am alone.

I am alone in a world filled with regret.

Filled with the thought of not loving myself to the full extent.

There are times when I feel like I am watching over myself,
Living a life full of regret.

I look down, having an out of body experience,
And feel horrible because of all the lies I have told.

"I am ok"

Is a statement I use all the time.

Not because I am "ok",

But because I cannot break the outer wall to show you
How I really feel.

I hide from the pain that causes heartache but
Loose myself in the process.

I tried so hard to be whole.
Turns out,
Being in pieces was more my journey.

Loving myself
Is one of the hardest things to do.

Every day I hide my true self.

I hide my
Thoughts, emotions, and ambitions

To satisfy the life of those
Who don't deserve me.

Most of the time,
I put others before myself.

Before my happiness.
Before my dreams.
Before my ambitions.

All to be taken advantage of
And gain nothing in return.

I never really knew
How much heartbreak and disappointment
My mind could take.
Until the day I had to leave.

I am the only one
Who can save myself
From my darkest thoughts.

But do I want to?

What does it mean to love yourself?

When I was little,
I always thought there were monsters under my bed.

I was wrong.

They all live in my head.

Everything is weighing on my mind and heart.

I feel, as if, I cannot breathe.

I feel like I need CPR.

Am I enough?

No, I am not dead.

But the light slowly slipped out of my eyes,

Causing the light within my soul to disappear.

My heart was stolen.
Not from someone who I gave my all to,
But from myself.

I stole everything from myself.

My heart, soul, and happiness.

Sometimes sadness can occupy your life.
But why does it have to occupy it for so long?

I look at everyone around me,
And realize that I haven't been happy for a while.

It just took a decade to realize it.

I have been damaged by all the pain I have experienced.
I feel like I am damaged goods.
I feel as if I never will escape the pain I have experienced.
Maybe one day I will.

Who knows where I will be in twenty years,
I just hope I am happy.

I'm empty and alone.

After everything I have been through,
I am still breathing.
Is it even worth the fight?

You are all traitors…

You left me in the dark alone with my thoughts.

That's probably the worst thing you could do to me.

You talked…

I listened…

I talked…

You left.

The shadows in my room are still lighter than my darkest thoughts.

Just say it,

"I'm broken."

I have been broken into pieces
And this time I don't think
I can put myself back together.

I started hating myself.
And I think I'm okay with it.

There are times when I think I made the wrong decision about leaving you.
But I feel if I didn't, I would hate you more than I hate myself.
And I just couldn't do that to you.

Don't act like I didn't love you.
I just didn't love myself.

I can't wait for the day where I can look back and say to myself,

"I can't believe it took so long for me to be in a place in my life where I'm actually happy."

Most days I feel…

Nothing.

Rarely, I feel something.

You can't break something

That's already broken.

I was supposed to be better than this.

But I'm not.

Even underneath the waves,
I am still breathing in a world
Where I am struggling.
I don't have the energy anymore to be the person you want
me to be.

Growing up I was never insecure about who I was.

Now?

I'm more insecure than ever.

I feel I am incapable of being loved.
It's terrible to think this but
I find it difficult to think otherwise.

I have lied to so many people,
That those lies became true in my own mind.

A constant reminder to myself:

"Don't forget to breath."

I'm not perfect.
But I deserve to be happy.

I am terrified to start over.
I would be starting from scratch.

But I think that's my only option.

I take every broken piece of myself

And leave them behind for someone to find,

So they can eventually save my life.

I build myself up
To tear myself down
Because I have only been
Comfortable in the dark.

I can be jealous sometimes.

Jealous that others are living in a world with their true self.

Jealous that I may never have the life they do because I don't want to disappoint those close to me.

I'm jealous of your happiness because all I have ever wanted was to be happy with who I am.

I have no idea
Who I am
Anymore.

Even as the sun seems so bright,
A dark cloud still occupies my soul.

A cloud that seems so dark and gray,
I seem to fade into the falling rain.

Enclosed in darkness throughout the light,
But having to push thru
Because people account for you.

That's probably one of the saddest things I have ever experienced.

I stand here
On the rail of a bridge I pass every day.

I'm standing here wondering
If anyone would truly miss me.

Not because people don't care about me,
But because no one really knows the true me.

I stand here,
Wanting to let go.

I am beautifully:

B
R
O
K
E
N

This house doesn't feel like my home.
I'm falling apart in a house, where I am not free.
Free from those who don't have my best interests at heart.

This house isn't my home, yet
I am stuck inside a house that isn't mine.

A house that has brought me closer to death.

I have spent too much time not moving on.

It's okay,
To not be okay.

I think I'm just too scared.

I'm scared I would be looked at different.

I'm scared they will be the judge and jury to my demise.

Losing the people close to me, would finally break me.

I am perceived as a person who has

No Feelings.

But in reality,
I am just that good at hiding them.

Perhaps I need to experience darkness
To appreciate light.

But how long do I have to be enclosed in darkness?

It cannot be perceived, touched, or heard.
It surrounds stars, fills voids,
And ends lives.

What am I?

I should be happy,
But this sadness,
comes from a place where
I can't find.

How are you doing?

Is a question I get asked time and time again
but I answer it with a lie that I can't unlearn.

Sometimes,
I feel too tired to try.

The hardest part?

Not being able to trust anyone enough to let go of all the bottled-up emotions I have held on to for so long.

It's easier to act like nothing is wrong so
you don't bring others down with you in the process.

In my mind,
I live a life where I have everything I want.
In reality, I have nothing.

All I have ever wanted was to feel something, anything.

My dreams do not consist of a perfect constructed life.
I simply just want happiness and heartache.
I just don't want to feel numb.

I have never felt a love where my heart skips a beat.
Where the butterflies are in the pit of my stomach.

I crave to feel a love like that.

I feel broken, bruised, and hurt.

I don't think I can ever escape this darkness.

My soul clings to my aspirations.

When I speak my thoughts no one seems to listen.
People hear me and my thoughts, but don't ever listen.

It's two a.m.
And I'm looking up at my bedroom ceiling,
Wondering where this darkness goes when I close my eyes.

It follows me in my dreams.

I'll come back to myself.

I'm standing and peering out of a window,
At a planet that I never anticipated becoming mine.
My spirit is weak
And my mind is gray.

I am trapped.
Trapped inside my mind.

Sometimes I'm scared of being the real me.
Not only because of what people will think about me,
But mostly because I'm scared that I won't have what I always dreamed of having.
You.

Being captivated by darkness has emptied my serotonin levels.

The aspect of ourselves
that is concealed within the depths of our nature
is known as our "dark side."

"Everything will be okay"
Is a phrase I use a lot.

It does not mean everything will lineup with the expectations you have set for yourself.

It means no matter the outcome of your life,
You'll discover that life is far richer and more significant than you could have ever dreamed.
Even if right now you are struggling.

It's crazy to think
I could have a life
where I am happy,
If I just sum up the courage to be true to who I am.

I am trying to be brave.
I am.

But I'm in this constant battle within myself.
Because of the judgment and looks others like me get.